MY FIRST LOOK AT PLANETS

NEPTUNE (TOP) IS FAR FROM THE OTHER PLANETS

Neptune

TERESA WIMMER

CREATIVE EDUCATION

Published by Creative Education

P.O. Box 227, Mankato, Minnesota 56002

Creative Education is an imprint of The Creative Company

Designed by Rita Marshall

Photographs by Bridgeman Art Library, Getty Images (Photodisc, Taxi), Photo Researchers

(Chris Butler / Science Photo Library, Victor Habbick Visions / Science Photo Library, Steve

Munsinger, NASA / Science Photo Library, NASA / Science Source, Science Photo Library,

Seth Shostak / Science Photo Library), Tom Stack & Associates (NASA / JPL)

Copyright © 2008 Creative Education

Printed in the United States of America

Library of Congress Cataloging-in-Publication Data

Wimmer, Teresa, 1975– Neptune / by Teresa Wimmer.

p. cm. — (My first look at planets)

Includes index.

ISBN-13: 978-1-58341-520-7

I. Neptune (Planet)—Juvenile literature. I. Title.

QB691.W55 2007   523.48'1—dc22   2006018251

First edition 9 8 7 6 5 4 3 2 1

NEPTUNE

LONELY PLANET

Up in the sky, far from Earth, is a **planet** called Neptune. People on Earth cannot see Neptune with just their eyes. They have to use a **telescope** to see it.

Neptune is part of the **solar system**. Besides Neptune, there are seven other planets. All of the planets move in a path called an orbit around the sun. Neptune is the farthest planet from the sun.

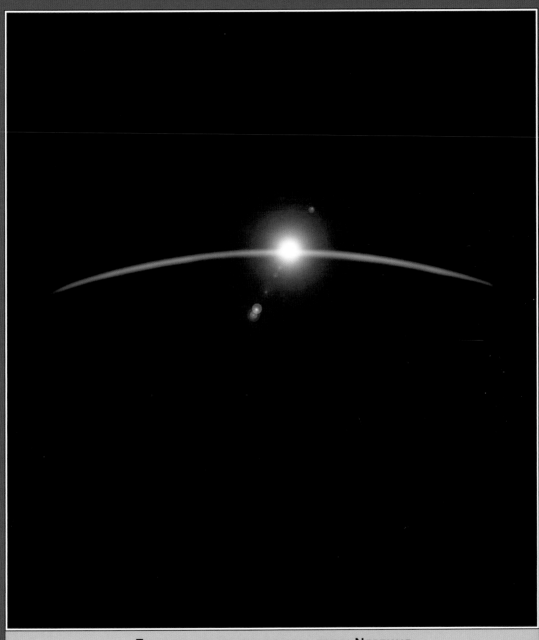

THE SUN LOOKS VERY SMALL FROM NEPTUNE

From Earth, Neptune looks like a tiny dot. But it is the fourth-biggest planet. Neptune spins like a top in the sky. It never stops spinning.

Blue and Cold

Neptune looks like a big ball, but it is made of **gas**. The gas makes it look blue. Thick clouds and fog cover Neptune. They make Neptune look pretty.

The days on Neptune

are short. One day

lasts for only 16 hours!

Neptune is far away from the sun's heat. That means it is a very cold place. Neptune is 10 times colder than a freezer! No people, animals, or plants live there. Breathing Neptune's gas would hurt them.

Neptune is a very windy planet. The winds have made three big storms. The biggest storm is called the Great Dark Spot. It has been blowing for a long time. The smallest

Neptune is always changing. The
storm spots and bright clouds
show up. Then they go away.

storm is called Scooter. It chases the other storms around the planet.

Rings and Moons

At least six rings circle Neptune. The rings look very dark. They are made of rocks and dust. Some of the rocks are as small as pebbles. Some are as big as Earth's moon!

Neptune has at least 13 moons. They move in an orbit around Neptune. A few of the

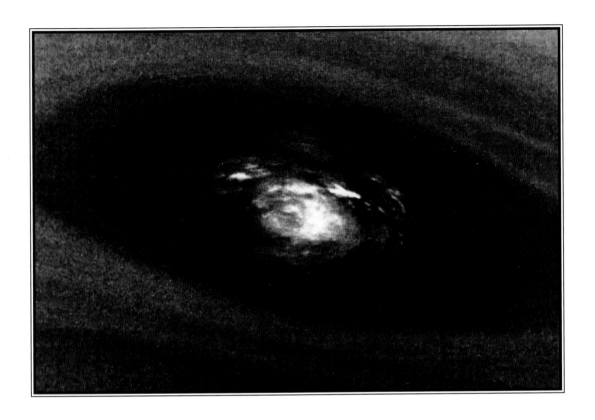

Some people think there
might be a big ocean
under Neptune's clouds.

Neptune's storms look like big, swirling spots

moons are big. Others are very small. Neptune might have more moons that people have not seen yet.

Neptune's biggest moon is named Triton. It looks pink with dark streaks. It is one of the coldest places in the solar system. Ice covers most of Triton's ground.

TRITON IS A VERY BRIGHT AND ROCKY MOON

People always want to learn more about Neptune. To see Neptune up close, people send **probes** there. The probes have special cameras. They take close-up pictures of Neptune. Then the pictures are sent back to people on Earth.

A few years ago, a probe flew by Neptune. The probe was called the *Voyager 2*. It took 12 years to get to Neptune.

It takes Neptune 165 years
to orbit the sun once! It
takes Earth only one year.

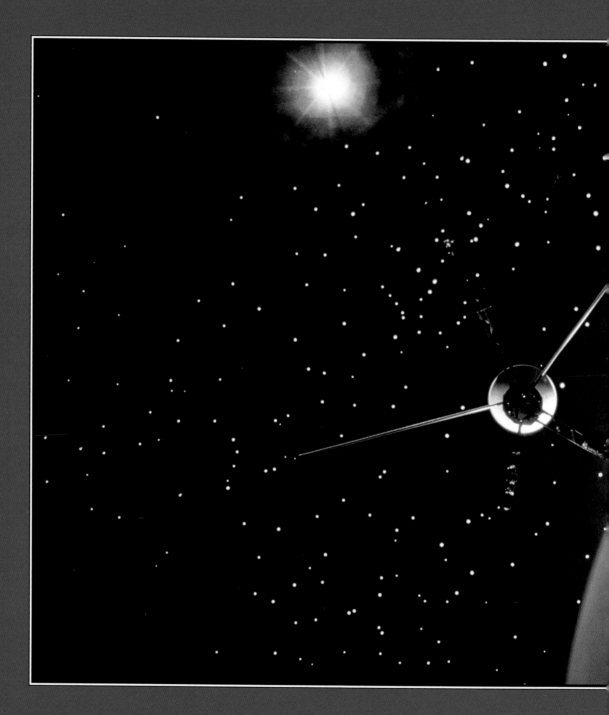

THE *VOYAGER 2* FLEW VERY CLOSE TO NEPTUNE

Voyager 2 took pictures of Neptune and its rings. It found more of Neptune's moons, too. One day, people will send stronger probes to Neptune. There are still many things to learn about this pretty, blue planet!

PROBES MAY TELL US MORE ABOUT NEPTUNE SOMEDAY

Hands-on: Make a Planet Neptune

Neptune is a pretty planet. You can make your very own planet Neptune!

What You Need

A big Styrofoam ball

A piece of yarn about eight inches (20 cm) long

Blue and brown markers

One gray, one brown, and two white pipe cleaners

Glue

What You Do

1. Color the Styrofoam ball blue. Leave a small, white spot near the middle (Scooter). Color a brown spot near the bottom (Great Dark Spot).
2. Glue the pipe cleaners around the middle of the ball in this order: white, gray, brown, white.
3. Glue one end of the yarn to the top of the ball.
4. Now you have your own planet Neptune!

NO ONE KNOWS WHAT GAS MAKES NEPTUNE SO BLUE

INDEX

WORDS TO KNOW

gas—a kind of air; some gases are harmful to breathe

planet—a round object that moves around the sun

probes—special machines that fly around or land on a planet or a moon

solar system—the sun, the planets, and their moons

telescope—a special tube that people look through to see faraway things up close

READ MORE

Chrismer, Melanie. *Neptune*. New York: Scholastic, 2005.

Rudy, Lisa Jo. *Planets!* New York: HarperCollins, 2005.

Vogt, Gregory. *Solar System*. New York: Scholastic, 2001.

EXPLORE THE WEB

Enchanted Learning: Neptune http://www.zoomschool.com/subjects/astronomy/planets/neptune

Funschool: Space http://funschool.kaboose.com/globe-rider/space/index.html?trnstl=1

StarChild: The Planet Neptune http://starchild.gsfc.nasa.gov/docs/StarChild/solar_system_level1/neptune.html